Novena to the holy soul in purgatory

A journey of Redemption and intercession for the holy souls in purgatory

Rev Spencer W. Nicholson

Table of contents

Introduction

In embarking upon this sacred novena, let us be ensconced in the sanctity of purpose that pervades our spiritual endeavors. The Novena Prayer for the Holy Souls in Purgatory stands as a venerable pilgrimage, a liturgical sojourn that transcends temporal boundaries and beckons the faithful to participate in the divine economy of mercy.

Purpose of the Novena

In the heart of this spiritual odyssey lies a purpose both venerable and profound. The Novena, as a sublime act of devotion, seeks to harness the efficacious power of prayer and intercession. Our purpose, guided by the teachings of the Church, is to extend a lifeline of supplication to the Holy Souls traversing the refining fires of Purgatory.

Through this purposeful endeavor, we engage in a sacred dialogue with the Communion of Saints, recognizing our role as intercessors for those who have departed from the temporal realm. It is an endeavor rooted in the salvific mysteries of our faith, where each prayer becomes a sacramental offering, invoking the mercy of our Triune God.

In contemplating the purpose of this Novena, we delve into the theological richness of purgatorial purification. Our prayers, woven with threads of empathy and understanding, become a balm for the souls yearning for the final embrace of divine love. The purpose, thus, transcends mere ritual; it becomes an act of profound charity and solidarity with the souls awaiting the Beatific Vision.

May this purpose be our guiding star, leading us through the luminous mysteries of redemption and into the celestial embrace of God's mercy. In the tradition of our faith, this Novena stands as a testament to the communion between the Church Militant and the Church Suffering, united in the sublime journey towards eternal communion with our Triumphant Lord.

Understanding Purgatory

Purgatory, a realm between heaven and earth, is a theological concept intricately woven into the tapestry of Catholic doctrine. It stands as a divine vestibule, where souls, having departed from earthly life, undergo a process of purification. This intermediate state, purgatorial in nature, is grounded in the mercy and justice of a loving God.

At its essence, Purgatory embodies the mercy of a benevolent Creator. It is not a punitive realm but rather a transformative passage, wherein the soul, marked by the remnants of sin, is cleansed and perfected. The Church teaches that nothing unclean can enter the presence of God, and Purgatory serves as the crucible for this sanctifying purification.

The understanding of Purgatory finds its roots in sacred scripture, particularly in passages that allude to a state where sins are forgiven but temporal consequences remain. This nuanced perspective underscores the continuity of God's redemptive plan, extending beyond the confines of earthly existence. It is a realm where God's justice meets His infinite mercy, allowing souls to be reconciled and prepared for the beatific vision.

Furthermore, the communion between the Church Militant and the Church Suffering is palpable in the concept of Purgatory. Our prayers and acts of charity can alleviate the temporal suffering of souls in this state, reinforcing the interconnectedness of the mystical body of Christ. This profound interplay underscores the Catholic understanding that the faithful are not isolated entities but part of a divine tapestry woven by the hands of Providence.

In contemplating Purgatory, the Catholic faithful are called to embrace a theology of hope. It is a hope grounded in the belief that, through the purifying fires of Purgatory, souls are readied for the sublime union with God. Our understanding of Purgatory, therefore, transcends mere doctrine; it becomes an invitation to participate in the divine drama of redemption, where God's mercy triumphs, and souls are ushered into eternal communion.

Delving deeper into the theological nuances of Purgatory, one encounters the profound wisdom of the Church Fathers and the rich tradition that has shaped this doctrine. It is a concept firmly rooted in the early teachings of luminaries such as St. Augustine and St. Gregory the Great. Their reflections emphasized the transformative nature of

Purgatory, wherein the soul undergoes a process akin to a refining fire, purging the temporal effects of sin while preserving the integrity of the soul itself.

The temporal nature of suffering in Purgatory is a crucial aspect of understanding this state. Unlike the eternal consequences of damnation, Purgatory involves a finite duration of purification. This aligns with the Church's recognition that, while forgiven through the sacrament of reconciliation, the soul may still bear the scars of sin that require healing. The image of purgatorial fire, not a material flame but a symbol of transformative purification, resonates with the understanding that God's love purifies and refines the soul.

Moreover, the theological foundation of Purgatory is intimately connected to the Communion of Saints. The Church Suffering, comprised of souls in Purgatory, is not separated from the Church Militant and the Church Triumphant. This interconnectedness is expressed through the practice of praying for the departed, offering indulgences, and engaging in acts of charity on behalf of the Holy Souls. It underscores the profound unity within the mystical body of Christ, where the pilgrim Church on earth collaborates with the Church in purification, fostering a bond that transcends the limitations of time and space.

In the grand tapestry of Catholic theology, Purgatory stands as a testament to the harmonious interplay of divine justice and mercy. It is an invitation to reflect on the unfathomable depths of God's love, which not only forgives sins but actively works towards the restoration and perfection of the soul. In contemplating Purgatory, we are beckoned to embrace a vision of the afterlife that resonates with the transformative power of God's redemptive plan, ultimately leading souls to their eternal home in the heavenly realms.

Understanding the Need to Pray for the Holy Souls

The imperative to pray for the Holy Souls emanates from a profound recognition of the interconnectedness within the mystical body of Christ. In the tapestry of Catholic theology, prayer for the departed is not merely a pious tradition but a duty rooted in charity and solidarity. The Church teaches that the bond between the Church Militant on earth, the Church Suffering in Purgatory, and the Church Triumphant in heaven is unbroken — a communion transcending the boundaries of time and space.

The souls in Purgatory, though assured of their eventual entry into heavenly glory, undergo a purifying process to cleanse the temporal effects of sins. Our prayers become a spiritual currency, a means of alleviating their purgatorial suffering and hastening their journey towards the Beatific Vision. This act of intercession mirrors the selfless love intrinsic to Christianity, where believers are called to bear one another's burdens and participate in the redemptive work of Christ.

Furthermore, the concept of praying for the Holy Souls underscores the Church's understanding of divine justice and mercy. While God's justice demands reparation for sins, His mercy provides a path for that reparation to be fulfilled through the prayers and sacrifices of the faithful. It is a recognition that the efficacy of prayer extends beyond the confines of earthly life, reaching into the realms of the afterlife where souls are in need of divine mercy and intercessory supplication.

In fostering a culture of prayer for the Holy Souls, the faithful not only contribute to the spiritual well-being of the departed but also cultivate a deeper appreciation for the transient nature of earthly existence. This practice instills a sense of humility and empathy, reminding believers that they too will one day rely on the prayers of those who remain behind. Thus, the need to pray for the Holy Souls is a sacred duty grounded in love, mercy, and a profound understanding of the eternal bonds that unite the pilgrim Church on earth with the souls on their journey to heavenly glory.

Final Preparation for the Novena

As we stand on the threshold of this sacred novena, let our hearts be attuned to the divine symphony that awaits. Final preparation is not merely a logistical endeavor but a spiritual discipline, a harmonious blending of intention, reverence, and anticipation.

In these moments of quietude, cultivate an interior disposition of receptivity. Allow the purpose of this novena, the purification and sanctification of the Holy Souls, to permeate your being. Let the spirit of charity guide your prayers, transforming them into fragrant offerings ascending to the heavenly realms.

Consider dedicating a sacred space for the duration of the novena. A quiet corner adorned with symbols of faith can become a sanctuary for focused prayer. Assemble the necessary materials—a prayer book, blessed candles, or sacramentals—to enhance the solemnity of your devotion. These tangible elements serve as reminders of the transcendent reality of the communion of saints.

Immerse yourself in the prayers and reflections that will unfold over the next nine days. Engage not only with the words but with the sentiments they evoke. Let the purpose of this novena be etched in your heart, compelling you to intercede fervently on behalf of the Holy Souls in Purgatory.

In the final moments before commencing, offer a prayer of surrender. Yield your intentions to the divine will, trusting in the providence of God. As you embark on this spiritual odyssey, may the grace of the Holy Spirit be your guide, and may the angels and saints accompany you on this journey of mercy, redemption, and profound communion. Amen

The Novena

Day 1: Invocation of Divine Mercy

Opening Prayer

Heavenly Father, source of boundless mercy and compassion, as we begin this sacred novena, we humbly gather in Your divine presence. Pour forth Your grace upon us, unworthy though we may be, as we invoke Your Divine Mercy on this inaugural day.

Lord Jesus Christ, Saviour of souls, we turn to You with contrite hearts, acknowledging our dependence on Your infinite love. As we embark on this journey of prayer for the Holy Souls in Purgatory, may Your merciful gaze pierce through the veils of purification, bringing solace and hope to those in need.

Holy Spirit, Advocate and Comforter, descend upon us as we lift our intentions before the throne of grace. Guide our words and sentiments, that our supplications may be pleasing in the sight of the Most High. Kindle within us a fervent desire to participate in the divine work of mercy, bridging the earthly realm with the celestial abode of Your boundless love.

Grant us the strength to persevere in this novena, fortified by the intercession of Mary, Mother of Mercy, and all the heavenly hosts. May our prayers resonate with the harmonies of the Communion of Saints, echoing through the realms seen and unseen.

In the name of the Father, and of the Son, and of the Holy Spirit. Amen.

Reflection on God's Infinite Mercy

In contemplating God's infinite mercy, we find ourselves standing on the precipice of divine compassion, a boundless ocean whose depths elude human comprehension. The very essence of mercy is woven into the fabric of God's character, an outpouring of love that knows no bounds. It is a mercy that transcends the limitations of our finite understanding, reaching into the depths of our brokenness with a healing balm that is both profound and transformative.

In the grand tapestry of salvation history, God's mercy unfolds as a resplendent masterpiece, revealing itself in the forgiveness bestowed upon repentant sinners, the parables of the Prodigal Son, and the sacrificial love epitomized on the Cross. Our reflections on God's infinite mercy invite us to dwell in awe and gratitude, acknowledging that His mercy is not a fleeting gesture but an eternal reality, beckoning us to return to His embrace.

As we embark on this novena, let us immerse ourselves in the ocean of God's mercy, allowing its waves to wash over the Holy Souls in Purgatory. In this reflection, we are called not only to receive this mercy but to become vessels of it, extending the divine compassion we have received to those in need. For in God's infinite mercy, we discover a source of inexhaustible grace, a wellspring that invites us to partake in the sacred dance of redemption.

Novena Prayer for Souls in Purgatory

O Merciful Lord, as we embark on this sacred novena, we lift our hearts in fervent prayer for the Holy Souls in Purgatory. In Your boundless compassion, look with kindness upon those who await the fullness of Your divine embrace.

Eternal Father, by the merits of Your Son's redemptive sacrifice, grant solace to the souls undergoing purification. May the refining fire of Your love cleanse them from all temporal consequences of sin, preparing them for the eternal splendors of Your heavenly kingdom.

Lord Jesus Christ, Good Shepherd of our souls, extend Your mercy to those who yearn for the radiant dawn of heavenly glory. As we offer these prayers, unite our intentions with the perfect sacrifice of Your Cross, that the Holy Souls may find rest in the shadow of Your redeeming love.

O Holy Spirit, Comforter and Advocate, intercede on behalf of these departed souls, and through our

*prayers, may they be swiftly ushered into the
eternal joy of communion with the Triune God.*

*Mother Mary, Star of Heaven, wrap these souls in
the mantle of your maternal care. With the angels
and saints, may they praise and adore the Most
Holy Trinity throughout the ceaseless ages. Amen.*

Day 2: Souls in Need of Healing

Opening Prayer

Heavenly Father, source of all healing and restoration, as we commence this second day of our novena, we turn our hearts towards the souls in need of your divine healing. In your infinite wisdom and compassion, look upon those undergoing purification with eyes of mercy and grant them the soothing balm of your love.

Lord Jesus Christ, Divine Physician, as we offer these prayers for the healing of the Holy Souls in Purgatory, may your healing grace penetrate the deepest recesses of their being. Heal the wounds of sin and imperfection, and may your redeeming love bring them consolation and strength on their journey toward eternal union with you.

Holy Spirit, our Comforter and Healer, descend upon us as we intercede for these souls in need. Infuse our prayers with the transformative power of your grace, that the healing they receive may radiate with the brilliance of your divine light.

Mary, Health of the Sick, join your prayers with ours, and envelop these souls in the mantle of your maternal care. May the heavenly chorus of intercession surround and uplift them, as we entrust them to the merciful embrace of the Holy Trinity. In the name of the Father, and of the Son, and of the Holy Spirit. Amen.

Reflection on the Healing Power of Prayer

In the tapestry of our spiritual journey, prayer emerges as a potent elixir, a channel through which the healing power of the divine flows into the depths of our souls. As we reflect on the healing nature of prayer, we are drawn into a sacred dance with the divine, where supplication becomes an intimate dialogue with the Author of all restoration.

Prayer, at its essence, is not merely a recitation of words but a profound communion with the Divine Healer. It is an invitation for the healing currents of God's grace to course through the wounds of sin and imperfection, bringing renewal and transformation. In our intercession for the Holy

Souls in need of healing, we become instruments of God's mercy, participating in the redemptive work initiated by Christ's sacrifice on the Cross.

The healing power of prayer extends beyond the temporal realm, transcending the limitations of earthly understanding. It is a spiritual force that reverberates through the fabric of our existence, touching the innermost recesses of the soul. As we lift our hearts in prayer for the souls in Purgatory, we tap into the reservoir of divine mercy, imploring the Divine Physician to mend the brokenness and bestow the fullness of healing grace.

In this reflection, let us be mindful of the profound truth that prayer is not bound by time or space. It is a timeless expression of our reliance on God's benevolence, a conduit through which His healing love flows ceaselessly. As we continue this novena, may our prayers be fragrant offerings, ascending to the heavenly throne and bringing solace to the souls in need of divine healing.

Novena Prayer for Healing Souls

Heavenly Father, Divine Physician, as we stand in the radiance of Your mercy, we lift our hearts in prayer for the healing of the souls in Purgatory. Look upon them with the compassion that knows no bounds and grant them the fullness of Your restoring grace.

Lord Jesus Christ, who bore our infirmities on the Cross, extend Your healing touch to these souls in need. May the wounds of sin and imperfection be healed by the balm of Your redeeming love. In Your mercy, console them and bring them the peace that surpasses all understanding.

Holy Spirit, Comforter and Source of Healing, descend upon us as we intercede for these souls. Infuse our prayers with the transformative power of Your grace, that the healing they receive may be a testament to Your abiding presence and love.

Mary, Health of the Sick, join your maternal prayers with ours, and enfold these souls in the mantle of your tender care. May our supplications rise like fragrant incense, offering comfort to the wounded and ushering them into the divine embrace of the Holy Trinity. In the name of the Father, and of the Son, and of the Holy Spirit. Amen.

Day 3: Hope and Redemption

Opening Prayer

Heavenly Father, source of unending hope and redemption, as we embark on this third day of our novena, we gather before you with hearts uplifted in anticipation of the divine gifts of hope and redemption. In your boundless mercy, infuse our spirits with the radiance of your love and guide us on this journey of prayer for the Holy Souls in Purgatory.

Lord Jesus Christ, our Beacon of Hope and Redeemer, illuminate the path of these souls with the brilliance of your saving grace. As we lift our hearts in intercession, may the flame of hope burn ever brighter within them, dispelling the shadows of purgatorial purification. Grant them the assurance of your redeeming love and the hope of eternal union with you.

Holy Spirit, our Paraclete and Fountain of Redemption, descend upon us as we offer these prayers. Pour forth your gifts of hope and redemption, transforming the hearts of the Holy

Souls and leading them towards the glory of your eternal kingdom.

Mary, Star of Hope, join your prayers with ours, as we entrust these souls to your maternal intercession. May the virtue of hope and the promise of redemption infuse our novena with grace, guiding these souls to the eternal joy found in the sacred heart of your Son. In the name of the Father, and of the Son, and of the Holy Spirit. Amen.

Reflection on Hope and Redemption

In the symphony of salvation, hope emerges as a celestial melody, resonating through the corridors of our existence. As we reflect on hope and redemption, we are beckoned to enter the divine narrative, where God's mercy transforms the discord of sin into a harmonious melody of redemption.

Hope, a radiant beacon in the spiritual firmament, is not a fleeting sentiment but an enduring virtue anchored in the promises of God. It is the conviction that, despite the shadows of purgatorial purification, the Holy Souls journey towards the radiant dawn of redemption. Our reflections invite us to embrace hope as a transformative force, a luminescent thread woven into the fabric of God's redemptive plan.

Redemption, the grand tapestry of God's love, unfolds through the sacrifice of Christ on the Cross. It is a divine exchange wherein the brokenness of sin is replaced with the healing balm of grace. As we contemplate redemption, we are called to recognize that every soul in Purgatory is a participant in this cosmic drama of salvation, awaiting the consummation of God's promise.

In our prayers for the Holy Souls, let hope and redemption be the wings that lift their spirits. As we intercede, we become ambassadors of God's promise, whispering into the ears of the departed the assurance that their journey leads not to eternal separation but to eternal union with the Author of their salvation.

May this reflection inspire within us a renewed sense of hope and an appreciation for the profound reality of redemption. In our prayers, let us infuse the souls in Purgatory with the grace to endure, the certainty of hope, and the joyful anticipation of the redemption that awaits them.

Novena Prayer for Souls Seeking Redemption

Heavenly Father, Fountain of Mercy, on this day of hope and redemption, we lift our hearts in prayer for the souls in Purgatory yearning for the fullness of your redeeming love. Look upon them with the eyes of compassion, and grant them the grace of joyful anticipation as they journey towards the eternal embrace of your divine mercy.

Lord Jesus Christ, our Redeemer, as we offer these prayers, extend the fruits of your salvific sacrifice to those souls seeking redemption. May the shadow of sin be dispelled by the radiant light of your love, and may the promise of eternal union with you inspire them with unwavering hope.

Holy Spirit, our Sanctifier and Guide, descend upon us as we intercede for these souls. Pour forth your grace of redemption, illuminating the path of purification and infusing their spirits with the hope that surpasses all understanding.

Mary, Mother of Hope, join your prayers with ours, as we entrust these souls to your maternal care. May the hope of redemption be a guiding star, leading them to the eternal splendor of your Son's presence. In the name of the Father, and of the Son, and of the Holy Spirit. Amen.

Day 4: Prayers of Intercession

Opening Prayer

Heavenly Father, as we enter the realm of intercession on this fourth day of our novena, we stand before you as humble advocates for the Holy Souls in Purgatory. In your infinite mercy, grant us the grace to offer prayers that bridge the temporal and spiritual realms, becoming vessels of intercession for those in need.

Lord Jesus Christ, our Mediator and Advocate, as we lift our voices in intercession, may your sacred heart be moved with compassion for the souls undergoing purification. Grant them the solace of knowing that they are not forgotten, as our prayers ascend like incense, enveloping them in the warmth of divine mercy.

Holy Spirit, our Intercessor and Comforter, descend upon us as we engage in this sacred duty of intercession. Guide our prayers, that they may be in harmony with your divine will, bringing comfort and relief to those who await the fulfillment of their purification.

Mary, Queen of Intercessors, join your prayers with ours, as we place before you the intentions of the Holy Souls. May our intercession be a sweet fragrance rising before the throne of grace, drawing down the divine mercy upon those who long for the prayers of the Church Militant. In the name of the Father, and of the Son, and of the Holy Spirit. Amen.

Reflection on Intercessory Prayer

Intercessory prayer, a sacred dialogue between the earthly realm and the divine, unfolds as a symphony of love and compassion. As we reflect on the profound act of intercession, we are drawn into the mystique of becoming instruments through which God's mercy flows to those in need.

At its core, intercessory prayer mirrors the very nature of Christ, who intercedes for us before the Father. It is an invitation to partake in the salvific mission of the Church, uniting our voices with the communion of saints and angels as we advocate on behalf of the Holy Souls in Purgatory. In this act, we enter into a sacred partnership with God, becoming co-laborers in the unfolding drama of redemption.

Intercessory prayer is not a passive supplication but an active participation in the divine plan. It is an acknowledgment that our prayers, like fragrant incense, ascend to the heavenly throne, touching the heart of God and invoking His mercy upon the souls we intercede for. Through this reflection, let us grasp the profound reality that our prayers hold the power to affect the destinies of those in need, becoming conduits for the outpouring of divine grace.

As we engage in intercessory prayer for the Holy Souls, let us be mindful of the transformative nature of this sacred act. May it deepen our sense of solidarity with the entire mystical body of Christ and kindle within us a fervent desire to be instruments of God's mercy in the world. In this ongoing dialogue of love, may our intercession be a beacon of hope, guiding souls towards the everlasting embrace of the Divine.

Novena Prayer for Interceding on Behalf of Souls

Heavenly Father, in this sacred hour of intercession, we bow before your throne of grace, lifting our hearts as advocates for the Holy Souls in Purgatory. Hear our supplications, O Lord, and through the merits of Christ's redeeming sacrifice, grant solace and relief to those souls in need.

Lord Jesus Christ, Divine Intercessor, we entrust to you the intentions of these souls seeking purification. May your sacred heart be moved with compassion as we, the Church Militant, intercede on their behalf. In your mercy, transform our prayers into a celestial chorus, resonating with the melodies of redemption.

Holy Spirit, our Guide and Advocate, descend upon us as we engage in this sacred duty of intercession. Inspire our prayers, that they may align with the divine will, becoming conduits for the outpouring of your healing grace upon the

Holy Souls. May our intercession be a fragrant offering, rising before the throne of mercy.

Mary, Mother of Intercession, join your prayers with ours, as we place before you the intentions of the Holy Souls. As the Queen of Heaven, intercede for them before the Holy Trinity, that they may experience the boundless mercy and love of God. In the name of the Father, and of the Son, and of the Holy Spirit. Amen.

Day 5: Offering Mass and Eucharistic Adoration

Opening Prayer

Heavenly Father, as we enter the sacred realms of Mass and Eucharistic Adoration on this fifth day of our novena, we stand in awe before the profound mysteries of your divine presence. In the hallowed silence of this moment, we offer our hearts as a living sacrifice, joining in the eternal liturgy of the heavenly hosts.

Lord Jesus Christ, present in the Most Holy Eucharist, we come before you with reverence and adoration. As we participate in the Holy Sacrifice of the Mass, unite our intentions with the perfect oblation of your own sacrifice on the Cross. May the Holy Souls in Purgatory receive the abundant graces flowing from this sacred banquet, and may their purification be hastened through the merits of this celestial offering.

Holy Spirit, our Sanctifier and Advocate, descend upon us as we enter into this Eucharistic encounter. In the sublime silence of Adoration, grant us the grace to contemplate the depths of your love and mercy. May our adoration become a fragrant incense, rising before the throne of the Triune God for the benefit of the Holy Souls.

Mary, Mother of the Eucharist, join your adoration with ours, as we place before you the intentions of the Holy Souls. May the Mass and Eucharistic Adoration be a source of divine consolation, drawing these souls ever closer to the radiant glory of your Son. In the name of the Father, and of the Son, and of the Holy Spirit. Amen.

Reflection on the Power of the Eucharist

The Eucharist, the summit and source of our Christian life, stands as a profound mystery that transcends human understanding. As we reflect on the power of the Eucharist, we are invited to enter into the sacred realm where heaven and earth converge, and the ordinary becomes extraordinary.

In the celebration of the Mass, we participate in the eternal sacrifice of Christ on the Cross. The bread and wine, through the miraculous transformation of transubstantiation, become the Body and Blood of our Lord. It is not a mere symbol but a sublime reality — Christ truly present among us. The power of the Eucharist lies in its capacity to unite us intimately with the divine, fostering a communion that goes beyond the limitations of time and space.

Eucharistic Adoration extends this encounter, inviting us to gaze upon the consecrated host with hearts open to the transformative love of God. In the silence of adoration, we find a sacred space where we can rest in the presence of the Eucharistic Lord. It is a moment of profound intimacy, where we can offer our adoration, supplications, and gratitude before the King of Kings.

The power of the Eucharist extends beyond the individual communicant. In the context of our novena, offering Mass and engaging in Eucharistic Adoration for the Holy Souls in Purgatory becomes a luminous act of charity. The graces bestowed through this sacramental encounter can be applied to alleviate the suffering of these souls, hastening their journey towards the radiant glory of God.

May our reflection on the power of the Eucharist kindle within us a deep reverence for this sacrament of love. As we partake in Mass and Adoration, may we be transformed by the divine presence, and may the fruits of this encounter bring solace and redemption to the souls in need.

Novena Prayer Offering Mass and Adoration for Souls

Heavenly Father, as we stand on the threshold of the divine mysteries of Mass and Eucharistic Adoration, we offer our hearts and intentions for the Holy Souls in Purgatory. In the holy sacrifice of the Mass, may the merits of Christ's passion and resurrection be applied to these souls, bringing them consolation and hastening their purification.

Lord Jesus Christ, present in the Most Holy Eucharist, we adore You with profound reverence. In this Eucharistic encounter, may the souls in Purgatory experience the transformative power of Your love. May the grace flowing from Your sacred heart bring them closer to the radiant glory of Your heavenly kingdom.

Holy Spirit, our Sanctifier and Advocate, descend upon us as we engage in this Eucharistic offering. Illuminate our hearts with the fire of divine love, that our prayers may become a fragrant incense before the throne of God, benefiting the souls for whom we intercede.

Mary, Mother of the Eucharist, join your adoration with ours, as we place before you the intentions of the Holy Souls. May the Mass and Eucharistic Adoration be a source of divine consolation, drawing these souls ever closer to the eternal embrace of the Triune God. In the name of the Father, and of the Son, and of the Holy Spirit. Amen.

Day 6: Consoling the Suffering Souls

Opening Prayer

Heavenly Father, on this sixth day of our novena, we come before you with hearts attuned to the cries of the suffering souls in Purgatory. In your infinite compassion, grant us the grace to be instruments of consolation, offering prayers that bring solace and alleviation to those undergoing purification.

Lord Jesus Christ, who bore the weight of our sins on the Cross, look with mercy upon the souls in Purgatory. May our prayers be a source of comfort, and may the consoling power of your love embrace those who yearn for the joy of eternal communion with you.

Holy Spirit, our Comforter and Advocate, descend upon us as we engage in this sacred duty of consoling the suffering souls. Infuse our prayers with the balm of divine mercy, that the souls in Purgatory may find relief and hope in the midst of their purification.

Mary, Consoler of the Afflicted, join your prayers with ours, as we place before you the intentions of the suffering souls. May our intercession be a soothing melody, echoing through the realms seen and unseen, bringing peace to those who await the fullness of redemption. In the name of the Father, and of the Son, and of the Holy Spirit. Amen.

Reflection on Consoling the Suffering Souls

In the quiet corridors of Purgatory, the souls in purification await the consoling touch of divine mercy. As we reflect on consoling the suffering souls, we are called to enter into the compassionate heart of God, becoming conduits of solace for those who yearn for the final embrace of heavenly glory.

Suffering in Purgatory is not a punitive sentence but a process of refinement, a journey towards the purity necessary for union with God. Our role in consoling these souls is an echo of Christ's own compassion, offering prayers and acts of charity that alleviate the temporal consequences of sin.

In our novena, we become pilgrims of mercy, walking alongside the suffering souls with hearts attuned to their silent pleas. Consolation is not just the alleviation of pain but the assurance that they are not abandoned, that the Church Militant remembers and intercedes on their behalf.

Mary, the Consoler of the Afflicted, exemplifies this role in the celestial realms. As we emulate her maternal care, our prayers become a gentle caress, soothing the wounds of those who endure the purifying fires. Consoling the suffering souls is an act of solidarity, a recognition that the mystical body of Christ spans across the realms of the living and the departed.

May our reflection inspire within us a renewed commitment to console the suffering souls. In our prayers and offerings, may the balm of divine mercy flow abundantly, bringing comfort to those in the crucible of purification. May our intercession be a beacon of hope, guiding these souls towards the radiant joy of eternal communion with God.

Novena Prayer for Consoling Souls in Purgatory

Heavenly Father, on this day dedicated to consoling the suffering souls in Purgatory, we lift our hearts in prayer and compassion. Look with mercy upon those who endure the purifying fires, and grant them the solace of your divine love.

Lord Jesus Christ, who suffered on the Cross for our redemption, extend the consoling power of your mercy to the souls in Purgatory. May our prayers and acts of charity be a source of comfort, alleviating their temporal pains and hastening their journey towards the eternal splendors of your heavenly kingdom.

Holy Spirit, our Comforter and Advocate, descend upon us as we engage in this sacred duty of consoling the suffering souls. Infuse our prayers with the balm of divine mercy, that the hearts of the departed may be lifted from the shadows of purgatorial purification.

Mary, Consoler of the Afflicted, join your prayers with ours, as we place before you the intentions of the suffering souls. May our intercession be a gentle embrace, bringing peace to those who await the fullness of redemption. In the name of the Father, and of the Son, and of the Holy Spirit. Amen.

Day 7: Acts of Charity and Mercy

Opening Prayer

Heavenly Father, as we embark on this seventh day of our novena, we come before you with hearts open to acts of charity and mercy. In your boundless love, guide us in deeds that reflect your compassion, offering solace and alleviation to the suffering souls in Purgatory.

Lord Jesus Christ, who taught us the way of love and mercy, inspire us to emulate your example in our actions. May the charity we extend to those in need become a tangible expression of your redemptive love, bringing comfort to the souls yearning for the embrace of heavenly glory.

Holy Spirit, our source of charity and compassion, descend upon us as we engage in acts of mercy. Infuse our deeds with the transformative power of your grace, that the temporal consequences of sin may be lessened for the souls we seek to aid.

Mary, Mother of Mercy, join your acts of charity with ours, as we place before you the intentions of the suffering souls. May our efforts be a reflection of your maternal care, bringing relief to those who await the fullness of redemption. In the name of the Father, and of the Son, and of the Holy Spirit. Amen.

Reflection on Acts of Charity

In the tapestry of our faith, acts of charity emerge as vibrant threads, weaving together the fabric of love that binds the mystical body of Christ. As we reflect on acts of charity, we are reminded that love is not merely a sentiment but a transformative force that transcends the boundaries of self, reaching out to embrace the needs of others.

Charity, born of love and nurtured by compassion, becomes a sacred vessel through which God's mercy flows into the world. It is an expression of our participation in the redemptive work of Christ, a tangible response to the call to love our neighbors as ourselves. In the context of our novena, acts of charity extend beyond the visible realm, becoming spiritual gifts offered on behalf of the suffering souls in Purgatory.

Our deeds of charity, whether small or grand, serve as bridges between the earthly and heavenly realms. They become whispers of hope and echoes of divine love, resonating in the corridors of Purgatory and offering solace to those undergoing purification. Acts of charity for the Holy Souls embody the very essence of Christian discipleship, reflecting the selfless love that Christ demonstrated on the Cross.

In our novena, let our reflections on acts of charity inspire us to reach out in love. Whether through prayers, sacrifices, or tangible deeds of kindness, may our charity become a source of consolation and relief for the suffering souls. As we extend our hands in love, may the light of Christ's mercy illuminate the path of redemption for those who await the fullness of heavenly joy.

Novena Prayer for Acts of Mercy Toward Souls

Heavenly Father, on this day dedicated to acts of charity and mercy, we offer ourselves as instruments of your love and compassion. Grant us the grace to extend acts of mercy toward the suffering souls in Purgatory, alleviating their temporal pains and hastening their journey towards the radiant glory of your heavenly kingdom.

Lord Jesus Christ, who taught us the way of love and mercy, inspire our deeds to reflect your redemptive love. May our acts of charity become a tangible expression of your boundless compassion, bringing comfort to the souls yearning for the embrace of heavenly glory.

Holy Spirit, our source of charity and compassion, descend upon us as we engage in acts of mercy. Infuse our efforts with the transformative power of your grace, that the suffering souls may find relief and hope through our charitable actions.

Mary, Mother of Mercy, join your acts of charity with ours, as we place before you the intentions of the suffering souls. May our deeds of mercy be a reflection of your maternal care, bringing solace and redemption to those who await the fullness of your Son's love. In the name of the Father, and of the Son, and of the Holy Spirit. Amen.

Day 8: Surrender and Acceptance

Opening Prayer

Heavenly Father, as we enter this eighth day of our novena, we come before you with hearts open to surrender and acceptance. In the quietude of this moment, grant us the grace to surrender our wills to yours and accept with humility the mysteries of your divine providence.

Lord Jesus Christ, who surrendered to the will of the Father on the Cross, guide us in the path of surrender and acceptance. May our journey of prayer for the suffering souls be marked by a profound trust in your mercy, acknowledging that your ways are higher than ours.

Holy Spirit, our Advocate and Comforter, descend upon us as we surrender our intentions for the Holy Souls. Grant us the grace of acceptance, recognizing that your plans are perfect and that our prayers, offered in surrender, align with the divine unfolding of redemption.

Mary, model of surrender and acceptance, join your prayers with ours, as we place before you the intentions of the suffering souls. May our surrender to your maternal care and acceptance of your guidance bring solace to those who await the fullness of redemption. In the name of the Father, and of the Son, and of the Holy Spirit. Amen.

Reflection on Surrendering to God's Will

Surrendering to God's will is not an act of resignation but a profound yielding of the soul to the divine providence that shapes the course of our lives. As we reflect on surrender, we are invited to release the grip of our own plans and embrace the sovereignty of God, trusting that His wisdom surpasses our understanding.

In the tapestry of our novena, surrender becomes a sacred offering, an acknowledgment that our prayers, hopes, and desires are ultimately subject to the divine order. It is an act of humility that places us in alignment with Christ, who surrendered

His own will in the Garden of Gethsemane, saying, "Not my will, but Yours, be done."

Surrender does not imply passivity; rather, it is an active entrustment of our intentions to the Author of all creation. It is an invitation for God's will to be woven into the fabric of our lives and our prayers. In the context of our novena for the suffering souls, surrender means recognizing that our petitions are offered in concert with God's eternal plan for redemption.

Acceptance is the companion of surrender, a disposition that allows us to receive God's will with open hearts. It is an acknowledgment that God's ways are beyond our comprehension, yet in His perfect love, He orchestrates the symphony of salvation. Acceptance is an act of faith, affirming that even in the mystery of suffering, God's mercy is at work, leading souls towards the brilliance of eternal joy.

May our reflection on surrendering to God's will inspire within us a spirit of abandonment to divine providence. As we surrender our intentions for the suffering souls, may acceptance be our response, trusting that God's will is a tapestry of love, woven with threads of mercy and redemption.

Novena Prayer for Souls Surrendering to God

Heavenly Father, on this day dedicated to surrender and acceptance, we come before you with hearts open to your divine will. In our surrender, we yield our intentions for the suffering souls in Purgatory, trusting in your infinite wisdom and mercy.

Lord Jesus Christ, who surrendered to the will of the Father for the redemption of humanity, guide us in the path of surrendering to your divine plan. May our prayers for the Holy Souls be marked by a profound trust in your mercy, acknowledging that your ways surpass our understanding.

Holy Spirit, our Advocate and Comforter, descend upon us as we surrender our intentions. Grant us the grace of acceptance, recognizing that your providence is perfect and that our prayers, offered in surrender, align with the divine unfolding of redemption.

Mary, model of surrender and acceptance, join your prayers with ours, as we place before you the intentions of the suffering souls. May our surrender to your maternal care and acceptance of your guidance bring solace to those who await the fullness of redemption. In the name of the Father, and of the Son, and of the Holy Spirit. Amen.

Day 9: Final Purification and Entrance into Heaven

Opening Prayer

Heavenly Father, as we stand on the threshold of this final day of our novena, we approach you with hearts filled with hope and anticipation. In your infinite mercy, grant the Holy Souls in Purgatory the grace of final purification, that they may be prepared to enter the eternal splendors of your heavenly kingdom.

Lord Jesus Christ, who conquered sin and death, be with the souls in their final moments of purification. May the redemptive power of your sacrifice on the Cross bring them the fullness of healing and restoration, preparing them to enter into the joy of your divine presence.

Holy Spirit, our Sanctifier and Guide, descend upon us as we offer our prayers for the Holy Souls. Illuminate their souls with the brilliance of your grace, guiding them through the final stages of purification and leading them into the eternal embrace of the Triune God.

Mary, Queen of Heaven, join your prayers with ours, as we place before you the intentions of the Holy Souls. May their final purification be swift, and may they enter into the radiant glory of heaven, where they will behold the face of God for all eternity. In the name of the Father, and of the Son, and of the Holy Spirit. Amen.

Reflection on the Final Purification

The final purification is the culminating phase of the souls' journey in Purgatory—a sacred passage marked by divine transformation and the purgation of every remaining imperfection. As we reflect on this crucial stage, we are reminded that God's mercy extends even to the final moments of purification, guiding souls into the radiant embrace of heavenly glory.

In the crucible of this purification, the souls experience the consummation of God's redemptive work. It is a profound encounter with the purifying flames of divine love, where every vestige of sin and imperfection is consumed, and the soul is refined to reflect the divine image in its fullness.

The final purification is not a punitive measure but a manifestation of God's desire to bring His beloved children into perfect communion with Him.

As we offer our prayers on this last day of the novena, we stand on the threshold of hope. Our intercession becomes a bridge that spans the realms, connecting the Church Militant with the Church Suffering. In our prayers, we implore the Holy Spirit to descend upon the souls, granting them the grace of swift purification and preparing them to enter the eternal joy of heaven.

Mary, as the Queen of Heaven, assumes a special role in our reflections. As a mother tenderly awaits her children, Mary intercedes for the souls with maternal love, accompanying them in their journey towards the beatific vision of her Son.

May our reflection on the final purification deepen our understanding of God's merciful plan. As we lift our hearts in prayer, may our intercession be a radiant light guiding the Holy Souls into the eternal splendors of heaven, where they will bask in the unending glory of the Triune God.

Novena Prayer for Souls Entering Eternal Glory

Heavenly Father, on this final day of our novena, we approach you with hearts filled with hope and anticipation. We lift our prayers for the Holy Souls in their final purification, that they may be swiftly prepared to enter the eternal splendors of your heavenly kingdom.

Lord Jesus Christ, conqueror of sin and death, be with the souls in their last moments of purification. May the redemptive power of your sacrifice on the Cross bring them complete healing, preparing them to enter into the joy of your divine presence.

Holy Spirit, our Sanctifier and Guide, descend upon us as we offer these prayers. Illuminate the souls with the brilliance of your grace, guiding them through the final stages of purification and leading them into the eternal embrace of the Triune God.

Mary, Queen of Heaven, join your prayers with ours. As the souls approach the threshold of eternal glory, may your maternal intercession accompany them, bringing comfort and assurance. May their entrance into heaven be swift, and may they behold the face of God for all eternity. In the name of the Father, and of the Son, and of the Holy Spirit. Amen.

Final Prayer

Heavenly Father, as we conclude this novena dedicated to the Holy Souls in Purgatory, we offer you our gratitude for the privilege of interceding on behalf of these beloved souls. In our prayers, may the purifying flame of your mercy hasten their journey towards the eternal radiance of your presence.

Lord Jesus Christ, our Redeemer, accepts our petitions for the souls in their final purification. May the merits of your passion and resurrection bring them healing and restoration, ushering them into the eternal joy of heavenly glory.

Holy Spirit, our Comforter, we entrust to you the souls we have prayed for throughout this novena. Illuminate their path with your grace, guiding them through the final stages of purification and leading them into the fullness of your divine light.

Mary, Queen of Heaven, we seek your maternal intercession. As the Holy Souls approach the threshold of eternal glory, may your tender care accompany them, bringing solace and peace.

In the name of the Father, and of the Son, and of the Holy Spirit.

Amen.

Made in the USA
Las Vegas, NV
11 October 2024

96662002R00036